50 Quick Ways to
Lea

By Mike Gershon

About the Author

Mike Gershon is known in the United Kingdom and beyond as an expert educationalist whose knowledge of teaching and learning is rooted in classroom practice. His online teaching tools have been viewed and downloaded more than 3.5 million times, making them some of the most popular of all time.

He is the author of over 80 books and guides covering different areas of teaching and learning. Some of Mike's bestsellers include books on assessment for learning, questioning, differentiation and outstanding teaching, as well as Growth Mindsets. You can train online with Mike, from anywhere in the world, at www.tes.com/institute/cpd-courses-teachers.

You can also find out more at www.mikegershon.com and www.gershongrowthmindsets.com, including about Mike's inspirational in-school training and student workshops.

Training and Consultancy

Mike offers a range of training and consultancy services covering all areas of teaching and learning, raising achievement and classroom practice. Examples of recent training events include:

- Assessment for Learning: Theory and Practice Keynote Address – Leigh Academies Trust Conference, London
- Growth Mindsets: Staff Training, Student Workshops and Speech to Parents – Longton Primary School, Preston
- Effective Questioning to Raise Achievement – Shireland Collegiate Academy, Birmingham

To find out more, visit www.mikegershon.com or www.gershongrowthmindsets.com or get in touch via mike@mikegershon.com

Other Works from the Same Author

Available to buy now on Amazon:

How to use Differentiation in the Classroom: The Complete Guide

How to use Assessment for Learning in the Classroom: The Complete Guide

How to use Bloom's Taxonomy in the Classroom: The Complete Guide

How to use Questioning in the Classroom: The Complete Guide

How to use Discussion in the Classroom: The Complete Guide

How to Manage Behaviour in the Classroom: The Complete Guide

How to Teach EAL Students in the Classroom: The Complete Guide

How to be an Outstanding Trainee Teacher: The Complete Guide

More Secondary Starters and Plenaries

Secondary Starters and Plenaries: History

Teach Now! History: Becoming a Great History Teacher

The Growth Mindset Pocketbook (with Professor Barry Hymer)

The Exams, Tests and Revision Pocketbook (from April 2016)

Also available to buy now on Amazon, the entire 'Quick 50' Series:

50 Quick and Brilliant Teaching Ideas

50 Quick and Brilliant Teaching Techniques

50 Quick and Easy Lesson Activities

50 Quick Ways to Help Your Students Secure A and B Grades at GCSE

50 Quick Ways to Help Your Students Think, Learn, and Use Their Brains Brilliantly

50 Quick Ways to Motivate and Engage Your Students

50 Quick Ways to Outstanding Teaching

50 Quick Ways to Perfect Behaviour Management

50 Quick and Brilliant Teaching Games

50 Quick and Easy Ways Leaders Can Prepare for Ofsted

50 Quick and Easy Ways to Outstanding Group Work

50 Quick and Easy Ways to Prepare for Ofsted

50 Quick Ways to Stretch and Challenge More-Able Students

50 Quick Ways to Create Independent Learners

50 Quick Ways to go from Good to Outstanding

50 Quick Ways to Support Less-Able Learners

And forthcoming in Summer 2016:

50 Quick Ways to Get Past 'I Don't Know'

50 Quick Ways to Start Your Lesson with a Bang!

50 Quick Ways to Improve Literacy Across the Curriculum

50 Quick Ways to Success with Life After Levels

50 Quick Ways to Improve Feedback and Marking

About the Series

The 'Quick 50' series was born out of a desire to provide teachers with practical, tried and tested ideas, activities, strategies and techniques which would help them to teach brilliant lessons, raise achievement and engage and inspire their students.

Every title in the series distils great teaching wisdom into fifty bite-sized chunks. These are easy to digest and easy to apply – perfect for the busy teacher who wants to develop their practice and support their students.

Acknowledgements

My thanks to all the staff and students I have worked with past and present, particularly those at Pimlico Academy and King Edward VI School, Bury St Edmunds. Thanks also to the teachers and teaching assistants who have attended my training sessions and who always offer great insights into what works in the classroom. Finally, thanks to Gordon at Kall Kwik for his design work and to Alison and Andy Metcalfe for providing a space in which to write.

Table of Contents

Introduction

Welcome to 50 Quick Ways to Support Less-Able Learners. We should begin by making it clear that we are not labelling a group of students as inherently less able. Rather, we are acknowledging that in any mixed-ability group some students will operate at a level below that of their peers. This does not mean they will always find themselves in that position. Nor does it mean that they will be in this position throughout their school career. The simplest example of this is the student who does well in certain parts of the curriculum but not so well in others.

Underpinning this book then, are three premises:

1) Every group of students contains some learners who perform at a level which is lower than that of their peers.

2) Every student has scope to grow, change, learn and develop.

3) Teachers are in a position to support their less-able learners, helping them to grow, change, learn and develop.

From these premises, a conclusion can be drawn:

- If we do things while we are planning, teaching and marking with the express intention of supporting our less-able learners, then it is likely they will make much better progress than if we don't set out with this aim.

The strategies, activities and techniques which follow give you the tools you need to support your less-able students. They are rooted in a sense of hopefulness and a belief that all students can make excellent progress, regardless of their starting point.

I hope you enjoy putting them into practice and giving your learners the best learning experience possible.

Teaching Up

01 Students respond to expectations. Expectations are both explicit and implicit. If we tell a student we would like them to work hard through the lesson, then we are stating an expectation explicitly. If we introduce challenging work on a regular basis but make no specific mention that we are doing this, then we are stating an expectation implicitly.

Teaching up means demonstrating implicitly that you believe less-able learners are capable of more. It is the converse of teaching down, which sends a negative message and should be avoided.

Almost without fail, students will live up or down to the expectations you convey to them.

Teaching up means presenting more challenging content and not dumbing down the lesson for less-able learners. Of course, we still scaffold, model, break ideas down, re-explain, offer support and so on. But this is done within the context of providing students with a learning experience which is challenging, stimulating and which implicitly communicates our expectation that they can achieve highly.

In short, teaching up is where you should start – and it is a theme which underpins this book.

Showing

02 Most communication in the classroom involves words – either verbally or written. Words need to be decoded, analysed and interpreted. For some less-able learners, the words they hear and see in the classroom can leave them feeling uncertain over what they need to do, or what they need to know.

Often, this is down to a lack of confidence. The learner struggles to back their own interpretations and, as a result, becomes reticent about starting work or doing what they think they should.

Showing the meaning of verbal and written communication gives these learners a supplemental way through which to access information. This means they can check how they have interpreted the words. If they can check, they can feel more confident.

Showing can involve:

- Physically modelling what you want students to do
- Using images on slide and handouts
- Using images to signal different task types
- Providing an example of what student work should look like
- Pointing students in the right direction

Eliciting Information

03 The more information you have about your less-able learners, the better. You can use this information to adapt your teaching so it closely meets their needs. Eliciting information about students' knowledge and understanding means diagnosing what they know and can do – as well as what they don't know and can't do. You can elicit information in a number of ways. For example:

- By asking questions
- By marking student work
- By observing students as they work
- By listening to students as they talk

You can also elicit information outside lessons by speaking to tutors, pastoral leaders and support staff. Gaining access to this information helps create a clear picture of where less-able learners are at. This places you in a better position to support them.

Those teachers who help their less-able learners to make the most progress invariably have an excellent understanding of who those learners are, what their strengths and weaknesses are, and what they respond best to in terms of support. This knowledge comes from the information they elicit inside and outside the classroom.

Questions Which Dig

04 Questions which dig are a good way to elicit useful information about student understanding. These questions see us chipping away at student thought. Our aim is to draw out as much of their thinking as possible. We want to provide a route through which they can articulate their ideas and knowledge – so that we can accurately assess where they are currently at and how they are thinking about the topic. Here are some questions which dig:

- Can you tell me more about that?
- What else do you think?
- Why do you think that? What examples do you have?
- What would you do in this situation?
- How might that change?
- Do you think it's easy or difficult?
- Do you think it's likely or unlikely?
- Do you think it will happen sooner or later?

Notice how the last three questions posit a choice. This is an extra technique you can use to elicit good information from less-able learners. Positing a choice in this way often makes it easier for the students to answer. Instead of having to pluck a response from the ether, they can instead hang their response on one of the two choices you have presented.

Verbalisation

05 Verbalising thought allows us to develop our thinking. This process of refinement is useful if we are seeking to understand:

- What we think about something

- An idea

- New information

To illustrate the point, consider the phrase 'Let's talk it through.' Why? Well, talking something through allows you to verbalise the disparate thoughts contained in your head. Through doing this you create order and coherency. This makes thinking easier.

Encouraging less-able learners to verbalise their thoughts means encouraging them to refine, edit, order and clarify their thoughts. Here are five techniques on which you can call:

- At the start of an activity, visit these learners in turn and talk to them about their thinking.

- Precede writing activities with a period of discussion.

- Pose a question and then invite students to discuss this with their partner for thirty seconds.

- Halfway through a task, visit your less-able learners and ask them to talk you through what they're going to do next.

- When these learners face a problem, discuss it with them. Use questions as prompts to help them verbalise their thoughts.

Analogies

06 Analogies are an explanatory tool in the classroom. They situate new information in the context of old information. For example:

- Black holes are like a super-powerful cosmic vacuum cleaner.

- A speech is like an advert – the aim is to influence the people who hear it.

- Deforestation is a bit like going bald – it totally changes the landscape and takes a lot of time, effort and money to reverse.

Analogies are a useful tool for supporting less-able learners. Call on them when explaining new ideas and information. In so doing, you will be taking advantage of the subtle benefit they bring.

Take the first analogy above. A less-able student may initially struggle to assimilate information about black holes. This information will likely be highly abstract and understanding it is partly contingent on understanding other things about physics and astronomy.

However, a less-able student will definitely know what a vacuum cleaner is. And this is how analogies work their magic. They let you take advantage of a student's prior knowledge. You can situate something new within the context of what students already know. This gives them a starting point – a way into the topic. Increased confidence will follow – which is the prerequisite for developing a more nuanced understanding.

Dividing Up The Cognitive Load

07 Working memory is limited to roughly seven piece of information, plus or minus two.

To demonstrate, take a moment to attempt to memorise the following numbers:

628

7301

6209736

724364519304

Chances are that you found memorising the first two fairly easy, the third one tricky and the last one very difficult.

Working memory is limited for all students. However, less-able learners will generally need to use their working memory for things more-able learners have secured in their longer-term memory.

For this reason, it is important that you divide up the cognitive load for them. That means you pay attention to how much students are having to do with their working memory. If this seems too much, break things up.

For example, an English teacher might set a task of planning and writing a news report. For their less-able learners they break up the cognitive load by asking them to:

- Talk about their ideas

- Make a note of three ideas they like

- Choose one idea to go with

- Note down three key things about this idea

- Write a short plan

- Write the first paragraph of the report

- Check this against their plan

- Carry on with the rest of the report

Here, the work is broken down into a series of separate tasks. Each one makes its own demand on working memory. Less-able students can do each one in turn, ensuring their working memory does not get overloaded (which might cause them to withdraw or give up).

Think – Talk – Do

08 This is a mantra you can teach your less-able students – one on which they can call in any activity, and which will help them to access the work by breaking up the cognitive load (see previous entry).

It is an order for doing things:

- Think – first we think about the question or activity.

- Talk – then we talk about our ideas with the teacher or a partner.

- Do – then we answer the question or start the activity.

This three step process divides up a piece of work. This makes it easier for students to access it. Having thought about things they are in a position to verbalise these thoughts. Having verbalised their thoughts they are in a position to put them into action.

Here is an example of the technique in a Geography lesson:

Teacher: Why might flooding be more likely if there are no trees on the hillsides?

Student – Think: Student considers what they know about flooding.

Student – Talk: Student turns to their partner and shares their thoughts. In the discussion they hear what their partner thinks and subsequently refine their own thinking.

Students – Do: Student is now in a position to provide an answer, based on the thinking and talking they've already done.

Encourage Questions

09 As we noted in Entries Three and Four, we can use questions to elicit information.

Another way to elicit information is by encouraging less-able learners to ask questions. This gives us an insight into their thinking. Particularly, what they find difficult or struggle to comprehend.

For example, a Religious Studies teacher might encourage their less-able learners to ask questions. In a lesson on Hinduism, they find these learners asking a whole series of questions about the religion. On reflection, the teacher would realise that these learners, for whatever reason, are starting off with a much lower base of prior knowledge regarding Hinduism than their peers.

This is exactly the kind of information we want. Without it, tailoring our teaching to support less-able learners is much harder.

Consider two teachers. The first actively encourages questions, the second discourages them. In the second classroom, there will almost certainly be a much bigger knowledge gap in the teacher's mind. They simply won't have the same level of access to what their less-able learners know, think, don't know and struggle to understand.

Peer Tutoring

10 The Education Endowment Foundation provides an online toolkit outlining the efficacy and average cost of various teaching and learning interventions. (educationendowmentfoundation.org.uk)

Near the top of their list of interventions is peer tutoring. This sees students tutoring each other and can take various forms:

- In a class, one student is assigned to tutor another.

- An older student is assigned to peer tutor a younger student, with this happening in class.

- An older student is assigned to peer tutor a younger student, with this happening outside of class. For example, in weekly intervention sessions.

In each case, the system is predicated on a more experienced or knowledgeable student tutoring a less experienced or less knowledgeable peer.

Using any of the three peer tutoring set-ups outlined above will help you to support your less-able learners. One thing to consider when setting up any peer tutoring is the relationship between tutor and tutee. To this end, try to pick out pairings of students you think will work well together, rather than just assigning pairs at random.

Regular Feedback

11 Feedback gives students access to your expertise. This expertise helps them to make progress. It tells them what they need to do next, what they need to change, or what they need to think about which maybe they haven't thought about so far.

It is for this reason that feedback is rated as one of the most important teaching and learning interventions (see Hattie, Visible Learning and the EEF Toolkit).

For less-able learners, regular feedback can have a big impact. This sees you returning to them regularly during the course of a lesson, either to give them new feedback based on what they have been doing, or to remind them of your initial feedback.

In the first case, the benefit comes from you directing students' thinking and actions through the course of the lesson; regularly moving them that little bit further on.

In the second case, the benefit comes from you reminding students about what they might have forgotten. Also, there is the added bonus that you and the student can discuss the feedback and how it links to the work they are currently doing.

Demonstrate how to Implement Feedback

12 If giving less-able learners feedback is the first step, demonstrating how to implement that feedback is the second.

Through demonstrating what implementation of your feedback will look like, you are modelling for students how to put your feedback into action. This makes it easier for them to do this. Your model acts as a starting point – something they can copy, imitate and then internalise.

If you do not demonstrate how to implement your feedback, then learners will have to work this out for themselves. They might be able to do this – or they might not. Why leave it to chance?

For example, a PE teacher might give one of her less-able learners the following piece of feedback: 'When you receive the ball I want you to watch it all the way into your hands. Don't take your eye off it. That will help make sure you catch it.'

She would follow this up by demonstrating what this looks like – and talking the student through it as she went: 'OK, Sally, watch my eyes as the ball's arriving. So I'm looking at it, now I'm following it as it gets closer. My hands open up and I'm still watching it, all the way into my hands.'

Precise, Specific Feedback

13 When you give feedback to less-able learners, make sure it is precise and specific. To illustrate why, compare these two pieces of primary-age feedback:

- I want you to check every sentence before you hand your work in. Make sure there is a capital letter at the start and a full stop at the end. If there isn't, I want you to change it so there is.

- You need to punctuate your work properly. Next time, make sure you check your punctuation before handing it in.

Both pieces of feedback say the same thing, but in different ways. The latter requires decoding – it requires the recipient to have prior knowledge of what correct punctuation is. The former is more precise and more specific. It tells the student exactly what they need to do, step-by-step.

The first piece of feedback is clear and unambiguous. The student will be able to implement it. The second piece lacks clarity and is somewhat ambiguous. The student may struggle to implement it.

Feedback of the first type is always to be preferred.

Active Repetition

14 Practice makes perfect. Repetition is an important part of all learning. Active repetition is the most effective form of practice. This is where the learner actively attends to what they are doing. It differs from passive repetition. That is where a learner practices without paying attention to what they are doing.

Active repetition is good for all learners. When it comes to less-able learners, it helps them to secure new knowledge and improve existing skills. Here are two examples of how to build active repetition into your lessons:

- Give less-able learners feedback followed by a set of similar questions or tasks. Show them how to implement the feedback and then leave them to have a go at this with the questions/tasks. Return 2-3 times during the activity to check how they are getting on. Use each occasion as an opportunity to redirect their attention to the practice in which they are engaged.

- Pose a question to the whole class and ask them to discuss it in pairs. Pair yourself up with a less-able learner and discuss the question with them. Ask a series of similar follow-up questions and then further question the student on their thoughts. This process is active repetition of thinking through repeated verbalisation of thoughts connected to a given topic.

Application Activities

15 Application is in the middle of Bloom's Taxonomy. First we have knowledge and comprehension, then application, then analysis, synthesis and evaluation.

Application activities are good for less-able learners for two reasons:

1) They are a form of active repetition (see last entry). This is because learners have to keep applying what they know and understand (knowledge and comprehension) to a series of different situations.

2) They are challenging – pushing students to go beyond simply remembering new information and ideas and what they mean.

When creating application activities, you can call on these Bloom's Taxonomy keywords:

Apply, Calculate, Choose, Demonstrate, Dramatise, Employ, Implement, Interpret, Operate, Perform, Practise, Role-Play, Sketch, Solve, Suggest.

For example:

- In each scenario, choose what you think is the best form of renewable energy to use and explain why.

- Suggest three ways the family could worship while they are on holiday.

- Use the design principles we discussed to sketch out an alternative design for the cereal packet, the glasses case and the sweet wrapper.

Model – Try – Return

16 Here's a mantra you can memorise and then turn to in any lesson. It will always help you to support your less-able learners:

- **Model** – model what you want your student to do; show them what success looks like.

- **Try** – ask your learner to try doing it for themselves. Give them space in which to do this.

- **Return** – Come back and ask the student to show you how they are getting on. Repeat your modelling or discuss their work with them.

And here's an example of what it looks like:

- **Model** – A History teacher works one-to-one with a less-able student. They show them how to analyse a source, demonstrating a five step process.

- **Try** – The teacher leaves the student to try analysing the source on their own. They decide to give them five minutes to work at it.

- **Return** – The teacher returns and asks the student to talk through their findings. The teacher notices the student has followed four out of the five steps. She praises the student, pointing to what they've done well, and then re-models the fifth step for them.

Discuss Application

17 In Entry Fifteen we looked at the benefits of using application activities. You may also have twigged that the previous entry (Model – Try – Return) was about student application (that is, applying what the teacher models for them).

It follows from these two entries that discussing application is helpful for learners. Why? Because it gives them a chance to reflect on what they have done, to think about the results of this, and to verbalise their experiences, thus reinforcing and further embedding them in their long-term memory.

You can discuss application activities with students one-on-one, or you can pose a question which they discuss with a partner. Here are some generic example questions, suitable for either approach:

- How easy was it to apply the ideas?

- When was it easier to answer the questions and when was it harder?

- Did your sketches turn out as you expected? Why?

And here are some example questions based on the application activities in Entry Fifteen:

- How did you decide which was the best form of renewable energy in each scenario?

- What made you suggest those three ways for the family to worship?

- How did the design principles influence each of your three designs?

Good and Bad Examples

18 Understanding what success looks like means having a clear sense of what you need to do to be successful. This is why we share success criteria with students.

Some less-able students may find that success criteria alone aren't enough. They may struggle to fully interpret these, seeing them as a decontextualized list of statements, instead of the clear explanation we intend.

In these situations, presenting a series of good and bad examples is the perfect way through which to provide context. Doing this attaches meaning to the success criteria, making it much easier for students to understand them and, therefore, to work towards them.

For example, we might have the following success criteria for a Citizenship presentation:

- The presentation should engage the audience and include at least one interactive element.

- You must give a succinct explanation and demonstration of each human right you have chosen to focus on.

- Slides should add to the presentation, not just repeat what you say.

Having explained these, we could then demonstrate what a good presentation would look like and what a bad presentation would look like. Doing this means we are modelling for students how to meet the success criteria as well as how not to meet them. This gives the criteria tangibility. It makes them more concrete, if you will, in students' minds.

Shared Success Criteria

19 You don't always have to define success criteria. Developing shared success criteria is an excellent way to empower students. Making them part of the process encourages a sense of agency – and a belief they can meet the challenge the criteria pose.

Here are three ways to develop shared success criteria:

- Before starting the task, ask students to discuss in pairs what outstanding work will look like. Use this as the basis of a whole-class discussion through which you agree on a set of three success criteria. These might be all-encompassing, or they might be the most important of many.

- At the start of the task, work one-on-one with a less-able learner. Discuss the success criteria with them and ask how they might tweak or change these. Agree between you a revised set of success criteria which the learner then seeks to meet.

- Mid-way through a task, ask your learners how happy they are with the success criteria. Maybe they're too easy – or maybe they're too hard. Through discussion come to a decision about whether the criteria need modifying. If they do, make these modifications together.

Genuine Praise

20 It's DT. You find DT a bit of a struggle. Your motivation is low and you don't really look forward to the lesson. When you're in there, you look around the room and see all your peers creating work which looks better than yours. Then the teacher comes over and, in an effort to be supportive, looks at what you've done and tells you it's amazing and that you're doing an absolutely fantastic job. How would you react?

Maybe like this: 'I don't believe him. I can see other people's work and what I'm doing isn't amazing.'

The point? All students can spot disingenuous praise a mile off. They don't want it. It doesn't help them. As soon as they sniff out the insincerity, they ask the question: Why would you give me insincere praise? Oh, because what I'm doing isn't very good. Because if it was good you'd give me genuine praise.

While students may not articulate their feelings in quite this way, it is a rough model of how they think.

So avoid disingenuous praise. While it's usually given with the best of intentions, it generally doesn't have a positive impact. Instead, look for opportunities to give genuine praise – once you start looking, you'll usually find them.

Break Tasks Down

21 Breaking tasks down mean simplifying them. The simplification stems from the fact that students only have one thing to think about at a time, instead of many. Here is an example:

Original Task:

Evaluate the arguments for and against Britain leaving the EU

Broken-down Task:

- Make a list of reasons for why Britain should stay in the EU

- Make a list of reason for why Britain should leave the EU

- Rank each list from most to least important

- Create an essay plan for the title: 'Evaluate the arguments for and against Britain leaving the EU.'

- Decide which arguments from each list you want to focus on

- Write your essay

More-able students will probably know that the original task entails the series of processes delineated in the broken-down task. However, many less-able students will struggle to make this judgement. As a result, they will find completing the task a little trickier. More importantly, they will find completing the task to a high standard much more difficult.

Providing a delineation such as we see above means doing a bit of the work for your students. They can then focus their attention on completing each step in turn – increasing the likelihood that they will make good progress and produce high-quality work.

Case Studies

22 Case studies make abstract ideas concrete. They embody concepts and, through their narrative construction, help students to assimilate new information. They also give students information about what an idea or series of ideas looks like in reality. This information can be used further down the line – it contributes to student understanding.

Here are three examples of case studies in action:

- **Topic:** Telling the truth. **Case Study:** The boy who cried wolf. **Impact:** Students can see the abstract concepts of lying and truth-telling embodied in the story. They also see the consequences which come from lying repeatedly and may infer the wider rule of trust in human relationships.

- **Topic:** Persuasive writing. **Case Study:** Speech by John F. Kennedy. **Impact:** Students can see specific rhetorical techniques in action. They can 'feel' the impact effective persuasive writing can have on an audience. They also get to see how certain elements of persuasive writing remain the same over time while others change.

- **Topic:** Gender Identity Disorder. **Case Study:** 15 year-old born with male sex chromosomes but who feels they are female. **Impact:** Students see an abstract idea contextualised in a real-life example. Students get an insight into the psychological impacts of the disorder on an individual. They also get to see how the definition of the disorder is applied in real life.

Mixed-Ability Groupings

23 Research by the Education Endowment Foundation suggests that setting and streaming have, on average, no impact on overall student achievement (google EEF Toolkit).

Mixed-ability groupings allow less-able students to learn from their peers. This can happen in all sorts of ways, including:

- Students are exposed to ideas and ways of thinking they might otherwise have missed.

- More-able students provide peer models. For example, through their speech, through how they think or through how they tackle questions and tasks.

- Students can turn to their peers for help and advice about their learning.

- Peers can teach each other. One of the major benefits here is that peers tend to use similar linguistic codes, which can allow them to explain ideas and information in a more accessible way than the teacher.

There are two ways to take advantage of the benefits of mixed-ability groupings. First, you can teach a mixed-ability class. This is not in your control and is dictated by the school and/or the timetable.

Second, when using group work you can ensure your groups contain a mix of abilities. This is in your control and is generally a good path to follow.

High Expectations

24 Right back in Entry One (Teaching Up) we outlined the importance of high expectations. There, we couched it in the terms of teaching up rather than dumbing down.

Here we can expand the idea a bit further.

Unfortunately, many less-able learners in a given subject or year group may have experienced low expectations through some or all of their school career. These expectations might have been communicated by their teachers, by their parents, by their peers or by a combination of these.

Often, students take on and internalise the expectations to which they are exposed. These external norms become internal norms. If a student has low expectations of themselves, they will likely make decisions which reflect this view when it comes to learning.

Consistently modelling high expectations means consistently providing students with a counterpoint to any prior experience they have had of low expectations. It means giving students a different story to tell about themselves as learners.

Perhaps the best way to do this is to treat every lesson as a blank slate. Regardless of what has happened before, this lesson is a new lesson in which every student can make outstanding progress. This assumption will then feed through into everything you do and say.

Defining High Expectations

25 Maintaining consistently high expectations is one thing, defining what this means is another.

In this situation, our first step is presenting less-able students with a different story they can tell about themselves as learners: That they are somebody who can achieve great things and make great progress; that they are somebody of whom learning and development is expected.

The second step is to turn this general sea-change in thinking into a series of specific, practical elements. By doing this we give students ways through which they can live up to our high expectations. First we change how they think, then we give them the practical tools they need to respond to this change.

Defining high expectations means coming up with a list of, say, five things you want to see from your students in every lesson. For example:

- You'll have a go at every question and every task. If you get stuck, you'll ask for help.

- You'll use the feedback I give you to learn more – and ask for extra feedback if you think you need it.

- You'll stick at things, even when they get tough, and ask for direction from me or a peer to help you overcome obstacles.

- You'll break up tasks so they are easier to do.

- You'll think about how you learn and keep using the techniques that work for you.

A list like this makes it easier for students to meet your high expectations. It demystifies them, giving students tangible things they can do in every lesson.

Concrete Questioning

26 Concrete questioning steers away from more abstract thought. For this reason, it is generally more accessible. You can use concrete questions when questioning less-able students. This will help you to:

- Check knowledge and elicit information
- Probe understanding
- Stretch student thinking, but not so far that they can't answer

Of course, you can bring in more abstract questioning later on as well. But concrete questioning is a great place to begin. Here are some examples of concrete questions (generally based on knowledge and comprehension):

- How many pigs were in the story and what houses did they live in?
- Who was Joan of Arc?
- What are three key features of an urban environment?
- How many ways can you pass the ball?
- What colour works best in this design?
- Should we use milk or eggs?
- Can you explain three sentences courts can give to offenders?
- When did Henry marry his third wife?

Contextualise Concepts

27 Concepts are ideas. They are intangible. They form the bedrock of our thinking. Courage is a concept. We can see someone being courageous, but we cannot go out and find courage in the same way that we can go out and find a chaffinch.

Contextualising concepts means connecting them to concrete examples. We touched on this idea in Entries Six and Twenty-Two (Analogies and Case Studies). By doing this, you make it easier for students to understand what a concept means. They can connect it to specific things, helping them to more clearly define its meaning and use.

Here are five further ways to contextualise concepts:

- Through stories. For example, Aesop's Fables contextualise ethical concepts.

- Through individuals. For example, Richard Branson can be used to contextualise the concept of entrepreneurship.

- Through exemplar work. For example, a write-up of an experiment can be used to contextualise the concepts of precision and accuracy.

- Through events. For example, the American Revolution can be used to contextualise the concept of political democracy.

- Through objects. For example, a Herman Miller chair can be used to contextualise the concept of ergonomic design.

Simplify

28 If one of your less-able learners is really struggling to get to grips with a task or question, simplify it.

This means giving them less to think about, less to do, or, something slightly different to think about or do.

Here are five ways to simplify questions:

- Rephrase the question. Say it in a way that makes it simpler.
- Turn a complex question into two simpler questions.
- Change the command word.
- Drop down a level on Bloom's Taxonomy.
- Use a simpler question stem.

And here are five ways to simplify tasks:

- Take something out of the task so students have less to do.
- Break the task up into a series of sub-tasks.
- Do part of the task for the student, then ask them to finish it.
- Provide a frame the student can use. Then they only need to think about content.
- Rephrase the task. State it in a simpler way.

Can't Yet

29 I can't do it. There's no way I can do that. I can't.

We've all heard these phrases. Less-able learners may be more apt to say them, due to finding the work more difficult than their peers.

Rephrase these statements. Show students a different way to think about what they can do:

- You can't do it yet.
- There's no way you won't be able to do it after we've worked hard at it together.
- You can't at the moment. That's natural. I couldn't do trigonometry the first time I tried. Let's work together then you'll be able to say you can.

In each case, our aim is not to deny the student's voice – that would be detrimental and unfair. Instead, we take what they have said and pose it back to them, reformulated. We demonstrate a different way to think.

This gives students an alternative; another way in which they can talk about their learning. If followed up by feedback, guidance and support, it also helps students to change what they can do.

Ignoramus Questioning

30 This questioning technique has a long history – stretching back at least as far as Socrates, Plato and Ancient Greece. It sees you playing dumb – acting the role of ignoramus. This has two benefits. First, it puts the onus on students to fully articulate their thinking – or to show you precisely what they mean. Second, it creates a sense of fun by inverting the traditional teacher-student relationship. Here are some examples of generic ignoramus questions:

- What does that even mean?
- I don't understand. Can you go back and start from the beginning?
- So, are you saying that…?

And here are some examples of specific ignoramus questions:

- But what is an atom? Can you tell me what an atom actually is?
- Where does rain come from, though? Is it magic?
- Why do buildings stand up? Are they glued together?

Ignoramus questioning is a great tool to have in your armoury. Enhance its impact by looking uncertain as you play the role!

Scaffolding

31 Scaffolding is where we take students some of the way. We give them a helping hand which makes it easier for them to complete the task, demonstrate a skill or answer a question. As you will have realised, many of the entries up to this point are specific examples of scaffolding.

Here are some more scaffolding techniques you can use to support less-able learners:

- Sentence starters
- Writing, reading and listening frames
- Visual glossaries
- Spelling tables
- Multiplication tables
- Crib sheets – for example, a crib sheet covering words, suffixes and prefixes which have Greek or Roman roots (these are often particularly hard for students to memorise)
- Checklists
- Questions to ask (e.g. of a source, before starting an essay; when facing a problem)
- Conversion charts (e.g. decimal to fraction)
- Dictionaries and thesauruses
- Half-completed work (e.g. a strengths and weakness table which already has two strengths and one weakness written in it)

Prompts

32 Prompting students means nudging them in a certain direction. This can help less-able learners to get started, to think differently, and to make connections between new information and prior knowledge.

For example, a Year 6 teacher might set his class off on an independent writing task, then circulate through the room and prompt his less-able learners into getting started by suggesting how they could begin.

Other examples of prompts include:

- Prompting students to make connections between lesson content and their wider experiences.

- Prompting students to break a question down into separate parts, making it easier to answer.

- Prompting students to look back in their books to see how they solved a similar problem last time.

- Prompting students to use keywords, techniques, or information they have already learned, earlier in the topic.

- Prompting students to use the success criteria to help them target their efforts.

Suggestions

33 If a less-able learner is struggling to begin a piece of work, struggling to answer a question or struggling to work out how to do something, why not make a suggestion to them?

This technique sees you putting an idea forward which the student can discuss with you, before deciding whether they want to take it on, adapt it to suit their thinking, or try something else altogether.

Your suggestion plays the role of both model and scaffold. A model because it shows the students what they might do. A scaffold because it gives the student something to think with, overcoming the uncertainty they have about what to do.

Here's an example:

- Freda, I can see you're thinking a lot about how to tackle translating the shape. Have you thought about using tracing paper to start off with, to make things a little easier? What do you think?

And here's another:

- Jamal, I noticed you're still planning your essay. Have you thought about using a shorter plan to save you time? What about if you cut it down to five bullet points? Do you think that might work?

Discuss Then Write

34 In Entry Five we looked at the benefits of verbalisation and touched briefly on using discussion as a prelude to writing. I want to come back to that here because it is such a powerful technique for helping less-able students to turn their thoughts into writing.

If you can get into the habit of always (or nearly always) preceding writing tasks with discussion – either in the form of a specific activity or just a brief bit of paired talk – you get into the habit of always (or nearly always) giving students the chance to articulate and refine what they want to say before they have to write it.

Don't forget that writing is a technology, passed on through culture. Speech, on the other hand, is a natural function of the human body, albeit one given shape and form through culture. This means students will nearly always be better speakers than writers.

Regularly preceding discussion with writing means giving students a chance to make mistakes, learn from these, edit their thoughts, refine their thoughts, and take advantage of their existing strengths. All of this makes the act of writing that bit more accessible.

You Tell Me

35 Less-able learners often lack confidence. One of the ways this can manifest itself is with students looking to the teacher for validation of their thinking and decision-making. For example, a learner who lacks confidence in Maths may frequently ask the teacher if they are doing the right thing. They want the teacher to confirm that the decisions they are making are the right ones.

Such desires are understandable. However, they are likely to inhibit learners over the longer term. Ideally, we want to get them into a position where they feel confident in themselves – and don't need external validation any more.

One technique you can use to achieve this comes in the form of the phrase: 'You tell me...'

Here's an example:

Student: Sir, am I doing it right?

Teacher: OK, let's have a look. Hmmm...well you tell me, Danny. What do you think? What made you choose this approach?

Notice how the teacher puts the onus back onto the student, giving them an opportunity to validate themselves. And if the student is doing things the wrong way, for whatever reason, this provides a great opportunity for teacher and student to discuss why this is a mistake – and what can be learned from it.

Trial and Error

36 Trial and error is one of the fundamental ways in which we learn. We try something out, see what happens, and make changes based on what we see.

Many less-able learners start to shy away from trial and error as they get older because they fear getting the answer wrong. This is bad. First, because they are cutting themselves off from a vital learning technique. Second, because they have developed a fear of mistakes and failure – when in reality both of these offer great opportunities to learn.

You can support less-able learners by promoting the use of trial and error and by minimising the costs of failure.

Here are three techniques for the former:

- Call it trial and improvement instead.

- Model how to use trial and error in your subject or with your age-group.

- Set up activities in which students have to try things out before getting to the right answer.

And here are three techniques for the latter:

- Turn mistakes into good mistakes and emphasise the learning they facilitate.

- Thank students when they make mistakes. Point out that if they hadn't made the mistake then you wouldn't have been able to teach away from it.

- Tell students that mistakes are evidence that the work you've set has the right level of challenge. (No mistakes = too easy)

Model How to Respond to Setbacks

37 All learners face setbacks. Some less-able learners find setbacks particularly difficult to deal with. Perhaps because they are low on confidence; perhaps because they have faced this experience more times than they would like during their school career.

How do you respond to setbacks? Positively, I'm sure.

So call on this and model it for your students. Show them how they too can respond positively to setbacks.

Examples of how you can do this include:

- Talking to students about a setback you faced and how you responded to this.

- Showing students your old school books, pointing out where you got things wrong and explaining how you responded to this.

- Giving students a three-step process to follow. For example: 1) Take a moment to compose yourself. 2) Look at what happened. 3) Ask what you can do differently. Walk students through this using the example of a specific setback they have faced.

- Coming up with a motto or slogan students can repeat to themselves whenever they face a setback (e.g. First Attempt In Learning).

- Asking older students to come and talk to your learners about how they deal positively with setbacks.

Show Me In Different Ways

38 Giving students different ways through which to demonstrate their knowledge and understanding means giving less-able learners the opportunity to self-select and to play to their strengths.

Here's an example of what it might look like in a Year 9 Citizenship lesson:

Task Question:

Do conflicts have the biggest impact on individuals, on families or on communities?

Options:

Choose one of the following options for your answer:

1. Write a report comparing the impact of conflict on the three groups.

2. Create a comic strip for each group showing how conflict can affect them.

3. Design a TV documentary which could give audiences an answer to the question.

4. Produce a speech persuading us of what you think the answer is and why.

5. Develop a leaflet which informs people about the impact of conflicts on each group.

Learners can look at the options and decide which one they would most like to attempt. This lets them choose something they feel comfortable with – increasing the likelihood they will produce high-quality work.

Copy and Adapt

39 Imitation often signals the beginning of learning. We see this throughout a child's development. Indeed, we notice it in ourselves when, as adults, we come to learn something new. Think, for example, about how you began to teach by, in part, imitating models of teaching with which you were familiar.

We can use this to our advantage when supporting less-able learners by asking them to first copy and then adapt. Here's an example:

- A PE teacher shows a group of less-able learners how to throw a long pass in rugby. She runs through the demonstration four or five times, then asks the group to pair up and copy her. After a few attempts, she gets the group back together, shows them again and, this time, highlights some of the mistakes they were making. She then asks them to get back into their pairs, to copy her once more but, this time, to adapt what they are doing so as to avoid the mistakes.

As you will note, this technique is a way of structuring practice, such that learners quickly come to understand how to do something – and how to do it well.

Diagrams

40 Diagrams are a particular form of visual information. They offer students insight into processes, relationships, connections and systems. They do not require decoding in the same way that written information does. Students can look at diagrams and fairly quickly assimilate the information contained within. They can also refer back to them with ease, during the course of an activity.

These reasons indicate why diagrams are a useful tool for supporting less-able students.

We can use them to convey information; students can use them for guidance and support during a task.

Here are five examples of the technique in action:

- A Chemistry teacher provides students with a diagram of a blast furnace alongside a written description.

- A Year 5 teacher gives students a diagram showing them how the solar system works.

- An English teacher gives students a diagram showing how key characters link in Romeo and Juliet.

- A Year 6 teacher provides students with a diagram showing how the different areas of the Maths curriculum connect together.

- A Geography teacher gives students a diagram illustrating coastal erosion, then plays them a video showing it happening in real life.

Teach Self-Regulation

41 Self-regulation is the process through which we keep ourselves on track, monitor our behaviour and direct our attention. A learner who is good at self-regulation is able to keep themselves focussed, notices if they stop paying attention and can use various strategies to help themselves to learn.

You can teach self-regulation to less-able learners. This gives them access to techniques they can use to improve their learning. Here are some examples:

- Sit down with a student and work together to identify warning signs which indicate they might be starting to lose focus. Then, come up with a way of responding positively to these.

- Show students the benefits of positive self-talk. This is where we say good things to ourselves in an effort to keep ourselves on task. It contrasts to negative self-talk, where learners tell themselves that they can't do things or aren't capable of achieving.

- Help students to understand the benefit of putting emotions to one side in the classroom. For example, talk to them about the difference between responding to a setback emotionally and responding to one by looking at what you could do to overcome it.

Work-Checking Techniques

42 Less-able learners may not know how to check their work before handing it in. Teaching them work-checking techniques means giving them a tool they can call on whenever they complete something. This helps them to spot mistakes, errors and omissions. It also helps to build their confidence – as they feel more in control of the process of completing and handing in their work. Here are three examples:

- A Food Technology teacher shows their less-able students how to taste the food they are creating as they go. They demonstrate the importance of assessing the level of seasoning, as well as how to correct any under- or over-seasoning they identify.

- A Year 4 teacher shows students how to check whether the sums they have completed are right. They demonstrate a technique the student can use again and again, as well as what to do if they find some of their calculations are incorrect.

- A Business Studies teacher shows their students how to work backwards through a cash-flow forecast to assess whether the calculations are correct. They deliberately include a mistake in their example and show students how to spot this – and how to correct it.

Decoding

43 Words need decoding. We need to know what they mean on their own and what they mean in context. For example: Egg. He has egg on his face.

The word 'egg' has multiple meanings. For many of us, the dominant meaning would be a chicken's egg – the food 'egg' which we eat. The sentence above illustrates how context modifies the meaning of words. Sometimes it adds meaning the word does not possess on its own. Sometimes it clarifies or specifies meaning.

In the above example, a certain knowledge of English idioms is required to understand the dominant interpretation of the sentence. That is, a figurative interpretation.

Less-able students sometimes struggle to decode the language they hear or see in the classroom. For example, they may struggle with words derived from Greek and/or Latin. Or, they may have only a vague notion of how to decode command words such as outline, evaluate and define.

Helping students to decode keywords and phrases means helping them to get a better handle on meaning – whether this is your meaning, the meaning of a text or the meaning of a question.

Record Progress

44 We all record progress, usually in our mark-books, where we track pupils' summative attainment. We may also record progress in formative terms. For example, by noting down student targets and the date on which they successfully achieve them.

Recording progress means you can track change over time. This, in turn, means you can spot patterns and trends. Crucially, you can use this information to make targeted interventions.

For example, you might notice on reviewing your mark-book that one of your less-able learners has plateaued over a period of months. This information gives you cause for concern. 'Why has this happened?' you wonder.

Only by recording and subsequently analysing progress are you in a position to make evidence-backed interventions. Doing this is important if you want to successfully arrest declines in less-able students' performance.

Given these students are starting from the lowest base in any given group, they are the ones likely to lose the most if a decline in performance is not spotted early. Hence why recording and analysing progress is key to supporting less-able learners.

Teach Reflection

45 Reflection helps students to reinforce learning. It also encourages metacognition and gives students a chance to refine their thinking.

Effective reflection needs to be taught. Just asking students to reflect isn't enough. After all, what does that actually mean for students, in tangible terms?

Here are two examples of how to teach reflection:

- At the end of a Year 10 Maths lesson the teacher leads a reflection. They ask students to think about three questions connected to the lesson. The teacher explains that these three questions will help students to think about what they've learned, how they learned it, and whether they used it successfully.

- At the end of a Year 5 Literacy lesson the teacher leads a reflection. They ask students to look back through their work and to identify the hardest part and the easiest part. They then ask students to explain to their partner why they made their choices, using their work as a prompt.

In both cases, the teacher is supporting the whole class, including their less-able students, by showing them how to reflect on specific things which formed part of their learning.

One-to-One Conversations

46 It isn't practical to have one-to-one conversations with every student you teach. However, using some of your time to have one-to-one conversations with less-able learners is always beneficial.

These conversations allow you to support those learners who most benefit from your interventions. It also sends a message to these students that you think they are important and want to help them as much as possible. This builds confidence and self-esteem. When engaging your learners in one-to-one conversations, try focussing on:

- What they are finding most difficult at the moment and why this is causing them problems.

- What successes they have had recently, why they were successful and how they can learn lessons from this to apply elsewhere.

- Their current understanding of the topic, including areas about which they remain uncertain.

- Talking about strategies and techniques they've been using in lessons recently, whether these have worked and what they might try next.

- Discussing what they want to achieve over the next term and how you can help them to achieve this.

Remembrance of Successes Past

47 Success is motivational. It is a reward for targeted effort and application of time and energy.

Less-able learners may experience fewer successes in the classroom than their peers. This can be demotivating for them. Some learners can even become disillusioned, particularly if they go for an extended period without seeing any reward for their efforts.

Reminding students of their past successes helps overcome this. It involves you priming students to think about the times they have succeeded which, in turn, helps them to remember the connection between effort, persistence and ultimate reward.

Sometimes you will need to make this connection really clear for students, as they may struggle to fully articulate it themselves. For example:

- I want you to keep working at this, Jamie. Remember when we were stuck on long division for weeks? You kept going, kept trying to apply the feedback I gave you – and eventually you succeeded. You can do the same again here.

Praise via School Networks

48 Delivering praise via school networks is a good way to draw attention to the hard work, progress and effort of less-able learners. This can be especially motivational as these learners may be less used to being rewarded in this way. Praise via school networks includes:

- Subject teachers telling form tutors about praise for a specific student in their form.

- Subject teachers telling heads of year or heads of house about praise for a specific student in their year/house.

- Subject teachers telling senior leaders about praise for a specific student they know pastorally or academically.

- Class teachers telling senior leaders about praise for a student in their class.

- Class or subject teachers putting students forward to receive praise in assemblies.

In each case what we are seeing is a public acknowledgement of the hard work and effort the student has been putting in. This is motivational – it is also a public attribution of status within the norms and values of the school.

Postcards Home

49 Another nice way to deliver praise is through postcards home. This sees you sending a postcard to a learner's house with a note on it indicating what they have done well recently. For example:

- A GCSE Psychology teacher might have a set of praise postcards they use to send messages home on a termly basis. They could use one of these to inform a learner's parents or carers about the progress they have made with a particular topic.

- A Year 3 teacher might have a set of postcards they use to praise effort and persistence. They could give these to parents who come to collect their children from school. In the process, they could draw parents' attention to what their child has done well and encourage them to keep praising this at home.

- A Year 7 form tutor might have a set of postcards they use to send parents of their tutees praise collated from subject teachers. For example, the tutor might email round their class's subject teachers asking for praise about different learners. They could then collate this and transfer it to the postcards before sending them off to parents.

Praise and Expect Effort That Has a Purpose

50 And so we reach the final entry in our journey. The last technique I can suggest to you for supporting your less-able learners and helping them to make the best progress possible.

Praising effort that has a purpose means praising the hard work students put in that is directed by the feedback you provide, the activities you set up or the questions you pose. In turn, this reinforces in students' minds that this is the kind of effort you want to see – and that this is what will help them to be successful.

Effort without a purpose is like running on the spot.

Effort with a purpose is like running towards the finish line.

You can use these metaphors to help students understand the difference. You can even turn them into common currency in your classroom, continually returning to them to remind students of what you and they are trying to achieve.

Of course, you can call on all of the techniques already mentioned in this book to help students target their effort – to give it purpose and direction. By doing this, and then praising the results, you'll go a long way to ensuring your less-able learners make excellent progress, grow in confidence and enjoy their time in your class.

So with that we conclude 50 Quick Ways to Support Less-Able Learners. Let me finish by wishing you good luck in your endeavours. The very fact that you are reading this book indicates that you want to achieve the best for your students. I hope the ideas, strategies and techniques I have outlined provide you with the means to do this.

A Brief Request

If you have found this book useful I would be delighted if you could leave a review on Amazon to let others know.

If you have any thoughts or comments, or if you have an idea for a new book in the series you would like me to write, please don't hesitate to get in touch at mike@mikegershon.com.

Finally, don't forget that you can download all my teaching and learning resources for **FREE** at www.mikegershon.com and www.gershongrowthmindsets.com

Printed in Poland
by Amazon Fulfillment
Poland Sp. z o.o., Wrocław